LEE-ENFIELD RIFLE NO. 4 MARK I *

Phantom Parts Diagrams & Parts Listing

MIDDLE COAST PUBLISHING

Middle-Coast-Publishing.com

Lee-Enfield Rifle No. 4 Mark I *
Phantom Parts Diagrams & Parts Listing

Middle Coast Publishing

ISBN-978-0934523-65-3
ISBN 0-934523-65-7

DEDICATION

This work is dedicated to Tommy and his rifle.

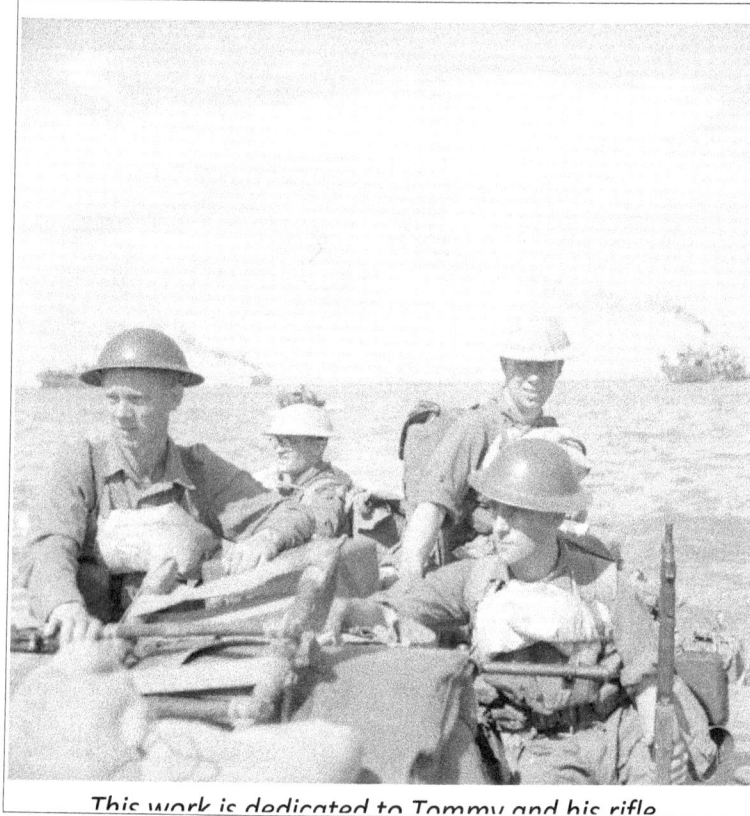

This work is dedicated to Tommy and his rifle.

CONTENTS

This publication contains detailed phantom drawings and parts identification lists by way of descriptive part names and parts number, for Rifle, .303 Calibre, Lee-Enfield, Rifle No 4, Mk 1 * along with its associated equipment. Illustrations show major assemblies, sub-assemblies and component parts.

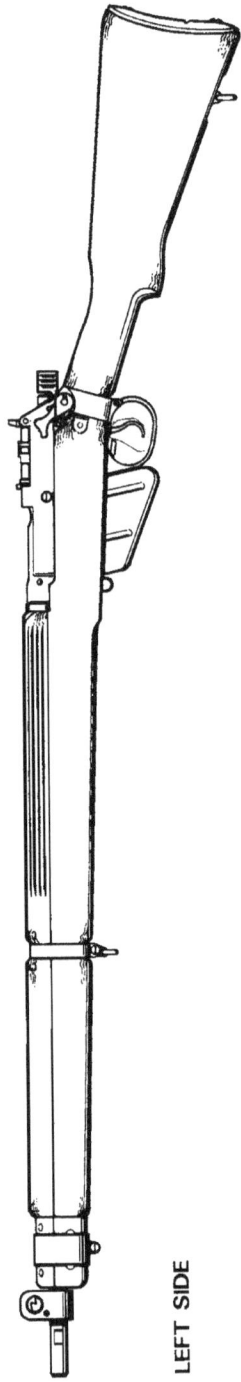

LEFT SIDE

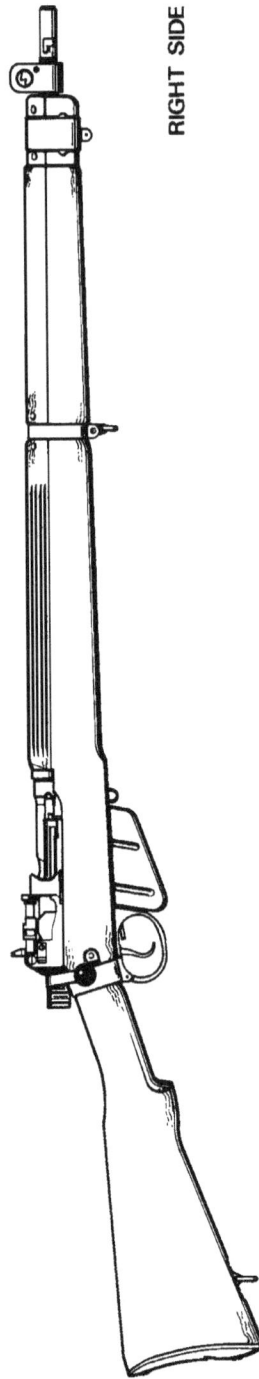

RIGHT SIDE

Illustration 1

ILLUSTRATION 1

INDEX #	NSN	DESCRIPTION
1	1005-21-107-2101	Rifle, .303 Calibre, Lee Enfield, No 4, and C No 4
1	1005-21-103-7587	Rifle, .303 Calibre, Lee Enfield, No 4, All Models
1	1005-21-103-1339	Rifle, .303 Calibre, Lee Enfield, No 4, Mk 1 *
1	1005-21-103-1341	Rifle, .303 Calibre, Lee Enfield, No 4, Mk 1 *
1	1005-21-808-9499	Rifle, .303 Calibre, Lee Enfield, No 4, Mk 1 *.Modified sporting/survival W/5 shot magazine, stock fitted W/recoil pad.
1	6910-21-116-7861	Rifle, .303 Calibre, Lee Enfield, No 4 Drill Pattern W/magazine.

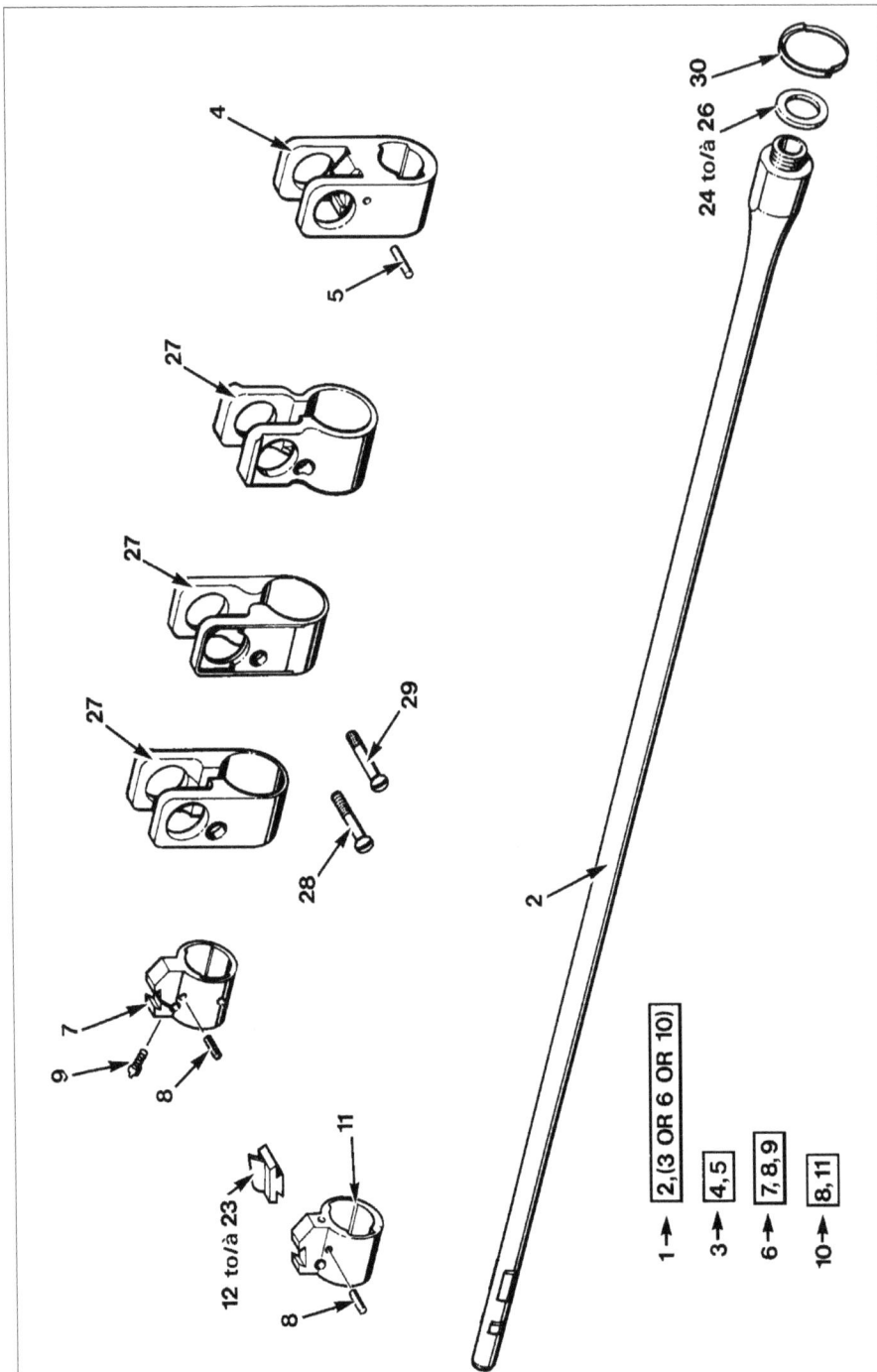

Illustration 2

ILLUSTRATION 2

INDEX #	NSN	DESCRIPTION
-1		Barrel Assembly Calibre .303
-2	1005-21-840-5515	Barrel, Calibre .303
-3		Bracket Assembly, Front Sight.
-4		Bracket, Front Sight
-5		Pin, Straight, Headless.
-6		Block Assembly Band, Front Sight, Mk 1.
-7		Block, Band, Front Sight, Mk 1
-8	1005-21-103-1124	Pin, Tapered, Plain. S, phos, 6.35 mm (0.250 in) taper per ft, 11.43 mm (0.450 in) nom lg, pin size 5/0, ends oval W 3.05 mm (0.120 in) nom rad.
-9	5305-21-107-1332	Screw, Special, Foresight
-10		Block Assembly, Band, Front Sight, Mk 2.
-11	1005-21-107-3085	Block, Band, Front Sight, Mk 2.
12	1005-21-103-4882	Blade, Front Sight. Minus 1.14 mm (0.045 in) C Mk 1, S, blued fin, blade 1.27 mm (0.050 in) w, sight 6.93 to 7.04 mm (0.273 to 0.277 in) h O/A, base 10.92 mm (0.430 in) w 9.02 mm (n) lg.0.355 i
-13	1005-21-103-4885	Blade, Front Sight. Minus 0.76 mm (0.030 in), S,
-14	1005-21-103-1111	Blade, Front Sight. Minus 0.38 mm (0.015 in), S,
-15	1005-21-103-1112	Blade, Front Sight. Zero, S, blued fin, blade 1.27 mm

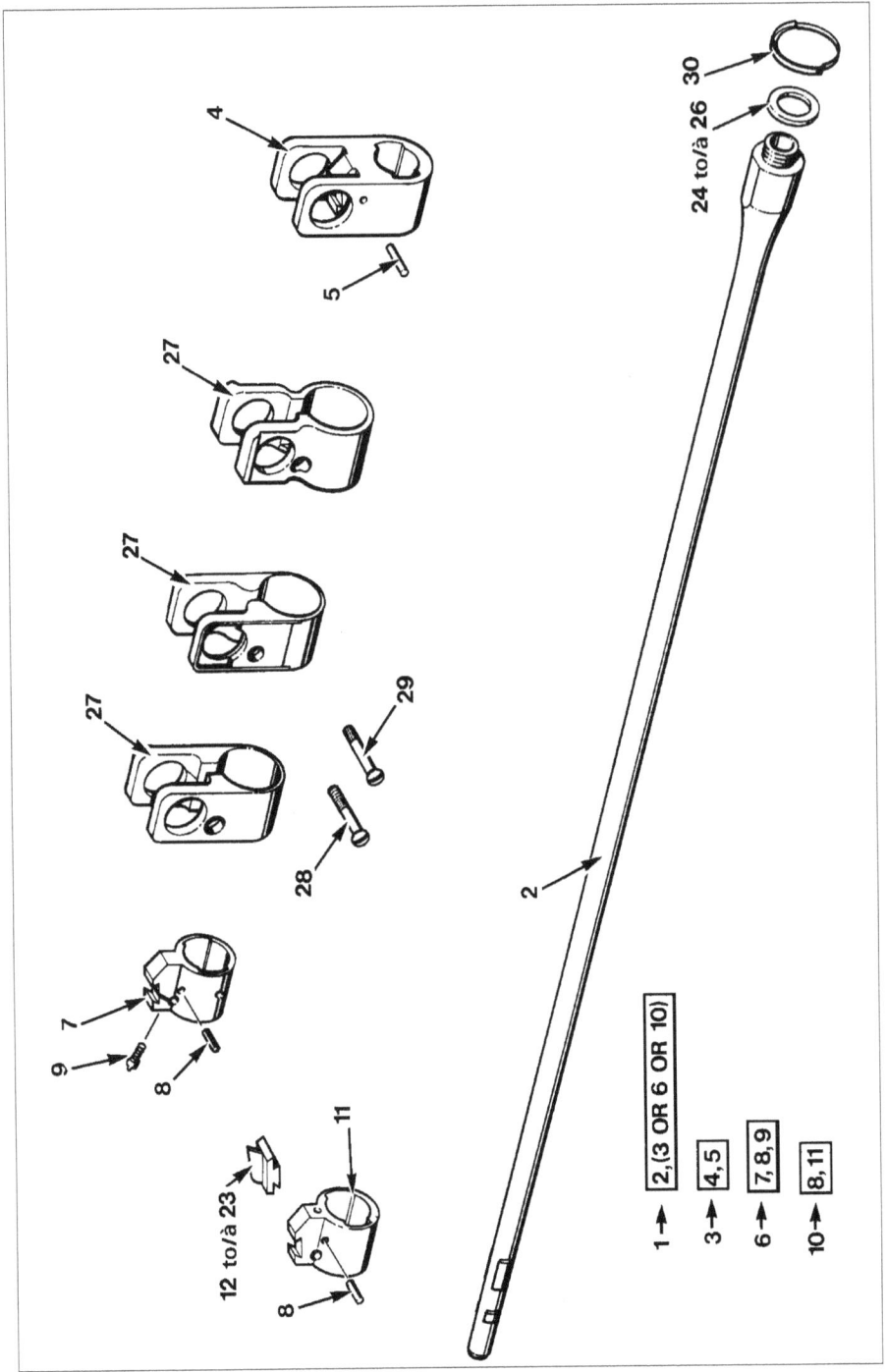

ILLUSTRATION 2

INDEX #	NSN	DESCRIPTION
16	1005-21-103-1113	Blade, Front Sight. Plus 0.38 mm, (0.015 in) S, blued fin, blade 1.27 mm (0.050 in) w, sight 8.46 to 8.56 mm (0.333 to 0.337 in) h O/A, base 10.92 mm (0.430 in) w 9.02 mm (0.355 in) lg.
17	1005-21-103-1114	Blade, Front Sight. Plus 0.76 mm (0.030 in), S, blued fin, blade 1.27 mm (0.050 in) w, sight 8.84 to 8.94 mm (0.348 to 0.352 in) h O/A, base 10.92 mm (0.430 in) w 9.02 mm (0.355 in) lg.
18	1005-21-103-1115	Front Sight. Plus. 1.14 mm (0.045 in), S, blued fin, blade. 1.27 mm (0.050 in) w, sight. 9.22 to 9.32 mm (0.363 to 0.367 in) h O/A, base 10.92 mm (0.430 in) w 9.02 mm (0.355 in) lg.
19	1005-21-103-1407	Blade, Front Sight. Plus. 1.52 mm (0.060 in), S, blued fin, blade. 1.27 mm (0.050 in) w, sight 9.60 to 9.70 mm(0.378 to 0.382 in) h O/A, base 10.92 mm (0.430 in) w 9.02 mm (0.355 in) lg.
20	1005-21-103-1116	Blade, Front Sight. Plus. 1.91 mm (0.075 in), S, bluedfin, blade. 1.27 mm (0.050 in) w, sight. 9.98 to 10.08 mm (0.393 to 0.397 in) h O/A, base 10.92 mm (0.430 in) w 9.02 mm (0.355 in) lg.
21	1005-21-103-4881	Blade, Front Sight. Plus. 2.29 mm (0.090 in), S, blued fin, blade. 1.27 mm (0.050 in) w, sight. 10.36 to 10.46 mm (0.408 to 0.412 in) h O/A, base 10.92 mm (0.430 in) w 9.02 mm (0.355 in) lg.
22	1005-21-103-4883	Blade, Front Sight. Plus. 3.05 mm (0.120 in), C Mk 1, S, blued fin, blade. 1.27 mm (0.050 in) w, sight 10.74 to 10.85 mm (0.423 to 0.427 in) h O/A, base 10.92 mm (0.430 in) w 9.02 mm (0.355 in) lg
23	1005-21-103-4884	Blade, Front Sight. Plus. 3.05 mm (0.120 in), C Mk 1, 11.43 mm to 11.23 mm (0.438 to0.442 in) h O/A, base 10.92 mm (0.430 in) w 9.02 mm (0.355 in) lg.
24		Shim. S, plain fin, 2.54 cm (1.000 in) ID, 3.18 cm (1.250 in) OD, 0.05 mm (0.002 in) thk mat.
25	5365-21-111-7248	Shim. S, plain fin, 2.54 cm (1.000 in) ID, 3.18 cm (1.250 po) OD, 0.08 mm (0.003 in) thk mat
26	5365-21-111-7247	Shim. S, plain fin, 2.54 cm (1.000 in) ID, 3.18 cm (1.250 po) OD, 0.010 mm (0.004 in) thk mat
27	1005-21-103-1401	Protector, Front Sight. (Mk 1 or Mk 2)
28	5305-21-106-8984	Screw, Front Sight Protector, screw, special, No 4 -BA x 21.59 mm (0.85 in) lg. 21,59 mm (0,85 po).....
29	5305-99-128-2156	Screw, Special, Guard, Trigger, Back.
30	1005-21-103-1200	Ring, Retaining, Rear Hand Guard.

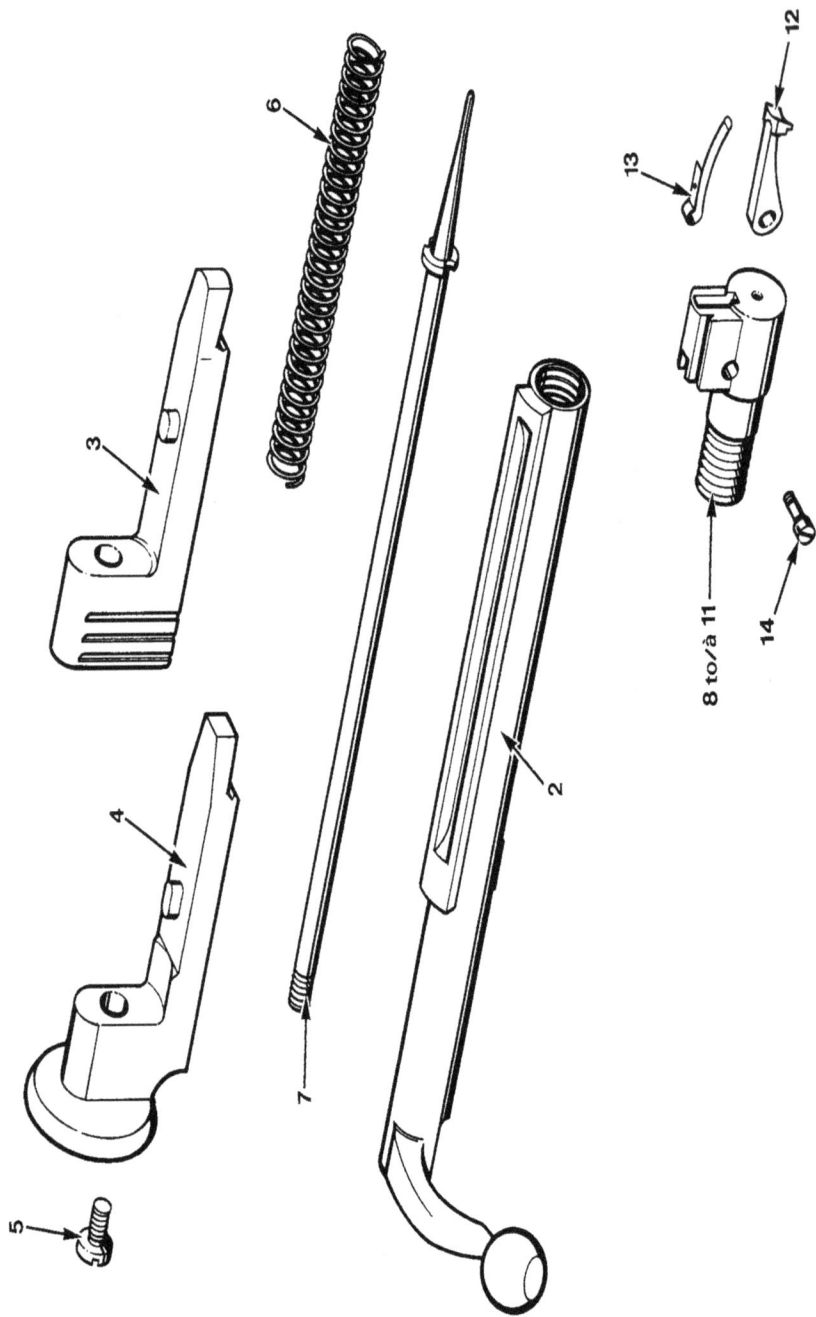

Illustration 3

ILUSTRATION 3

INDEX #	NSN	DESCRIPTION
-1	1005-21-113-7654	Bolt Assembly, Breech.
-2	1005-21-103-1330	Bolt, Breech. S, blued fin, 14.12 cm (5.560 in) O/A lg.
-3	1005-21-103-1235	Cocking Piece. C Mk 2
-4	1005-21-113-8096	Cocking Piece. C Mk 1.
-5	5305-21-107-1214	Screw, Machine, fil hd, D, anti-rust fin, No 4-BA, 6.35 mm (0.250 in) fas lg.
-6	5360-21-103-5538	Spring, Cocking Piece. Spring helical, compression, S, tinned, 6.65 mm (0.262 in) ID, 8.66 cm (3.410 in) free lg, 0.61 mm (0.024 in) mat dia 30-1/2 coils, must work freely in 9.22 mm (0.363 po) dia bore and over 6.40 mm (0.252 po) dia rod.
-7	1005-21-860-3785	Firing pin
-8	1005-21-103-1143	Head, Breech Bolt, No 0.
-9	1005-21-103-1144	Head, Breech Bolt, No 1.
-10	1005-21-103-1145	Head, Breech Bolt, No 2.
-11	1005-21-103-1146	Head, Breech Bolt, No 3.
-12	1005-21-103-1337	Extractor, Cartridge.
-13	1005-21-103-1121	Spring, Cartridge Extractor.
-14	5305-99-128-2155	Screw, Special, Cartridge Extractor. N° 5 – BA, 7.62 mm (0.30 in) lg.

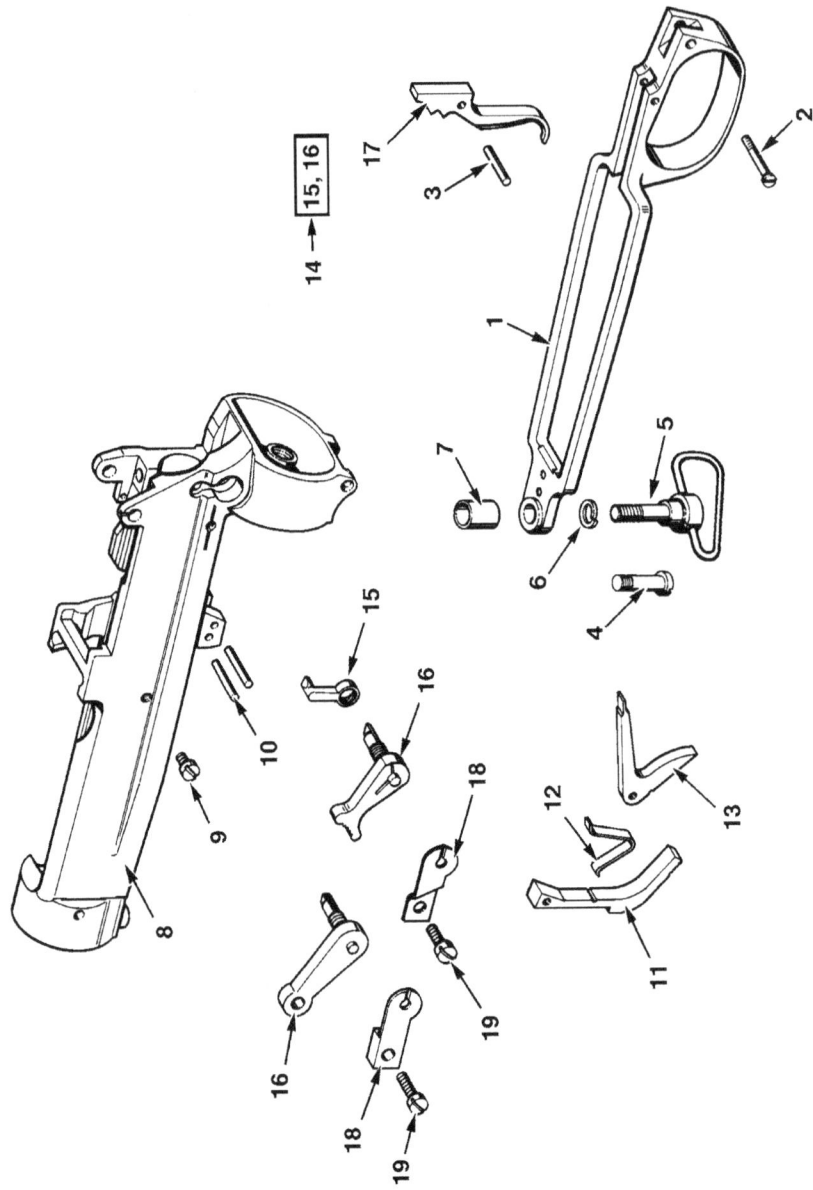

Illustration 4

ILLUSTRATION 4

INDEX #	NSN	DESCRIPTION
-1	1005-21-103-1134	Guard, Trigger. S, 15.80 cm (6.220 po) max O/A lg.
-2	5305-99-128-2156	Screw, Special, Guard, Trigger, Back.
-3	5315-21-106-6931	Pin, Straight, Headless. S, anti-rust fin, case hardened, 3.66 mm(0.144 in) nom dia, 15.47 mm
-4	5305-99-128-2158	Screw, Special, Guard, Trigger, Front.
-5	1005-21-103-1202	Swivel, Small Arms Sling. S, loop opening 2.84 cm
		(1.120 in) nom w 17.27 mm (0.680 in) nom h, fas
		3.66 cm (1.440 in) O/A lg 22.86 mm (0.900 in) thd lg,
		26 thd/ in. UNC. (No 4, Mk 1 * (T) only)
6	5310-00-933-8121	Washer, Lock, split helical ring, right hand, corrosion resisting steel, PASS, 6.48 mm (0.255 in) min 6.78 mm (0.267 in) max ID, 12.42 mm (0.489 in) max OD,
		1.19 mm (0.047 in) min 1.48 mm (0.057 in) max mat thk.
-8	1005-21-103-1230	Body, Rifle, Mk 2.
-9	5305-99-128-2278	Ejector screw hardened, 3.66 mm (0.144 in) nom dia, 19.30 mm (Qty 1 for No 4, Mk 1)
-12	1005-21-103-5451	Spring, Sear.
13		Sear, S, 4.45 cm (1.750 in) lg O/A, 6.32 mm (0.249 in) w. O/A.
14		Locking Assembly, Bolt
15	1005-21-113-7692	Catch, Safety.
16	1005-21-113-7677	Bolt, Locking.
17	1005-21-103-1142	Trigger.
18	1005-21-103-1201	Spring, Locking Bolt. (2 models)
19	5305-21-107-1331	Screw, Machine. Fil hd, S, phos ctd, No 3 BA.

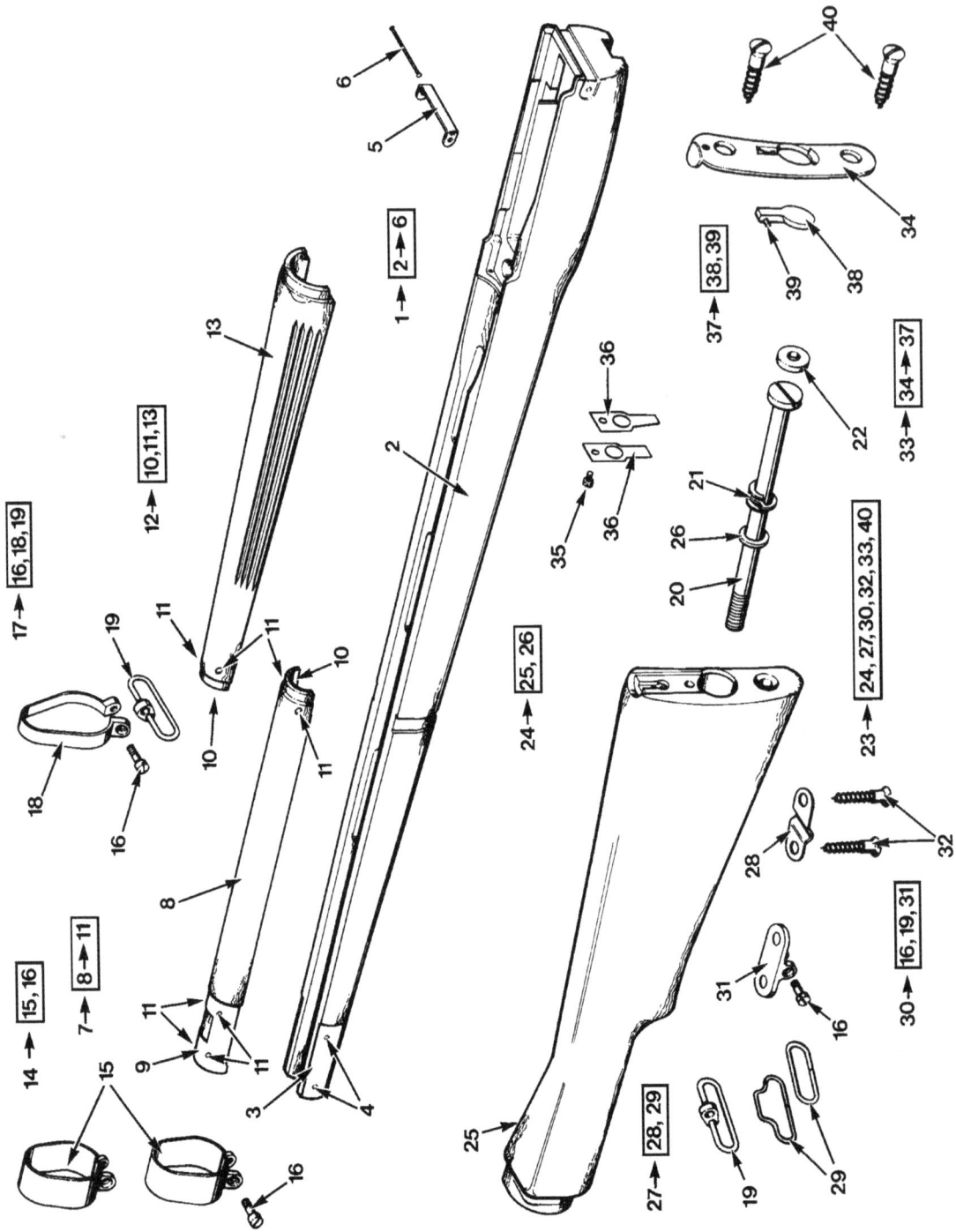

Illustration 5

ILLUSTRATION 5

INDEX #	NSN	DESCRIPTION
-1	1005-21-103-1206	Stock Assembly, Fore-end. Pin, Straight, Headless. S, anti-rust fin,..... 3.66 mm (0.144 in) nom dia,..... 3.06 cm (1.203 in) nom lg, oval ends W 3.05 mm (0.120 in) nom rad.
2	1005-21-116-5050	Stock, Fore-end. walnut or beech 71.53 cm (28.160 in) l lg
3	1005-21-103-1210	Cap, Stock, Fore-end.
4	5315-21-106-6933	Pin, Straight, Headless.
5	1005-21-113-7797	Tie Plate
6		Rivet, Tie Plate.
7	1005-21-103-1138	Guard Assembly, Hand, Front
8		Guard, Hand, Front. walnut or beech
9		Cap, Front Hand Guard.
10		Liner, Hand Guard. S, 0.56 mm (0.022 in) thk, semi-circular W/2 holes 2.49 mm (0.098 in) dia.
11		Rivet, Tubular, Flat Head, Drilled Shank. S, no surface treatment, shk in. dia 6.35 mm (0.250 in) lg, hd 2.39 mm (0.094 in) dia 0.71 mm (0.028 in) h. (For alternate use NSN 1005-21-113-8133)
12	1005-21-103-1139	Guard Assembly, Hand, Rear.
13		Guard, Hand, Rear. Walnut or beech, 27.81 cm (10.950 in) lg O/A.
14	1005-21-113-8072	Band Assembly, Small Arms Sling Swivel, Upper.
15	1005-21-103-1208	Band Assembly, Small Arms Sling Swivel, Upper.
16	5306-21-106-0535	Bolt, internally relieved body. fl fil hd,0.282 in. nom dia,0.121 in. nom h; slot dr; stl; 4.7x0.8ba thd;0.250 in. min thd lg; 0.520 in. nom fastener lg; 0.078 in. nom conc hole dia; special feat: type b anti rust finish.
17	1005-21-113-8073	Band Assembly, Small Arms Sling Swivel, Lower.
18	1005-21-103-1204	Band, Small Arms Sling Swivel, Lower. S, 9.91 mm (0.390 in) min 11.18 mm (0.440 in) max lg, 4.96 mm (1.953 in) h, W/screw type fas.
19	1005-21-103-1214	Swivel, Small Arms Sling. S, opening 3.33 mm (1.310 in) w, 8.13 mm (0.320 in) h, 14.22 cm (1.662 in) O/A hg, 4.85 mm (0.191 in) dia swivel mounting hole.
20	5305-99-123-7587	Screw, Machine. 7/16 (11.11 mm)-14BSW, 12.50 cm (4.920 in) lg.
21	5310-99-961-8260	Washer, Special, Spring Stock.
22		Washer, Non-Metallic. Leather 7.94 mm (5/16 in) ID, 19.84 mm (25/32 in) OD, 3.18 mm (1/8 in) mat thk.
23		Stock Assembly, Butt, Bantam. (includes items 24 to 32)
24	1005-21-103-1236	Stock, Gun, Shoulder, Bantam. Walnut, 31.24 cm (12.300 in) lg, 12.14 cm (4.780 in) w.
25	1005-21-113-1490	Stock, Gun, Shoulder. Bantam.
23	1005-21-113-8062	Stock Assembly, Gun, Shoulder. Long.
24	1005-21-103-1234	Stock, Gun, Shoulder. Long. Walnut 35.03 cm (13.800 in), lg 12.14 cm (4.780 in) w.
25	1005-21-113-1424	Stock, Gun, Shoulder. Long.
23		Stock Assembly, Gun, Shoulder. Normal. (includes items 24 to 32)
30	1005-21-103-1233	Stock Assembly, Gun, Shoulder. Normal. (includes items 24 to 32)
25	1005-21-113-7773	Stock, Gun, Shoulder. Normal
23		Stock Assembly, Gun, Shoulder. Short. (includes items 24 to 32)
24	1005-21-103-1232	Stock, Gun, Shoulder, Short. Walnut, 35.51 cm (12.800 in), lg 12.14 cm (4.780 po) w.
25	1005-21-113-7789	Stock, Gun, Shoulder. Short.

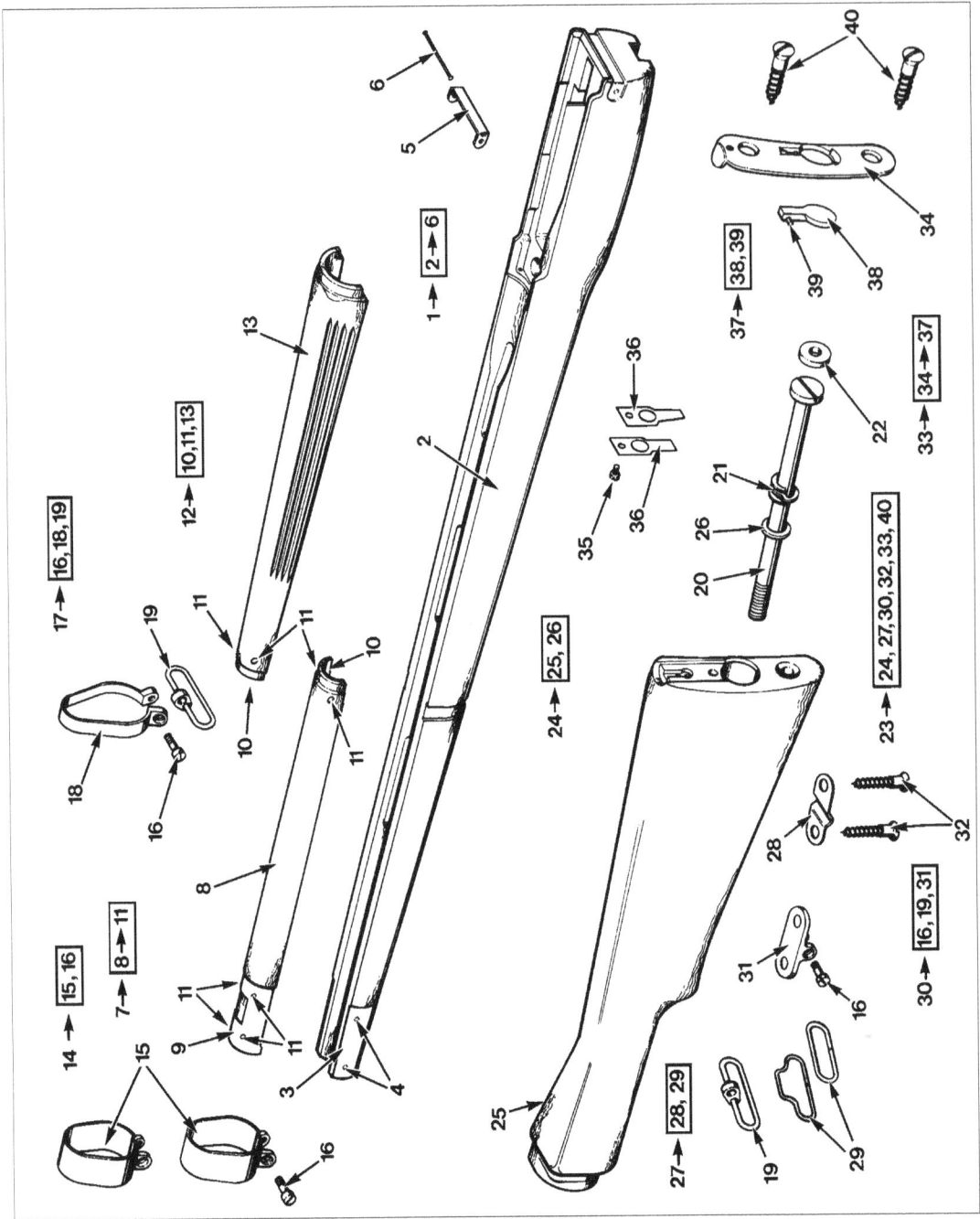

ILLUSTRATION 5

INDEX #	NSN	DESCRIPTION
26	5310-00-809-4085	Washer, Flat. Rd shape, rd hole, S, phos, 11.89 mm (0.468 in) ID, 23.39 mm (0.921 in) OD, 1.65 mm 0.065 in) mat thk.
27	1005-21-113-8066	Bracket Assembly, Rear Sling Loop.
28	1005-21-103-5587	Bracket, Rear Sling Loop.
29	1005-21-103-558	Swivel, Small Arms Sling. S, opening 3.33 mm (1.310 in) w, 17.78 mm (0.700 po) h, 4.23 mm (1.666 in) O/A lg. (2 styles)
30	1005-21-113-7688	Bracket Assembly, Rear Sling Loop.
16	5306-21-106-0535	Bolt, internally relieved body. fl fil hd,0.282 in. nom dia,0.121 in. nom h; slot dr; stl; 4.7x0.8ba thd; 0.250 in. min thd lg; 0.520 in. nom fastener lg; 0.078 in. nom conc hole dia; special feat: type b anti-rust finish.
19	1005-21-103-1214	Swivel, Small Arms Sling. S, opening 3.33 mm (1.310 in) w, 8.13 mm (0.320 in) h, 14.22 cm (1.662 in) O/A hg, 4.85 mm (0.191 in) dia swivel mounting hole.
31	1005-21-103-1209	Bracket, Rear Sling Loop.
32	5305-00-062-7893	Screw, Wood, oval countersunk hd, slot dr, S, blued, No 10 wood, 3.18 cm (1.250 in) fas lg.
33	1005-21-103-1207	Plate Assembly, Butt, Shoulder, Gun Stock. Sub item NSN 1005-21-107-3086.
34		Plate, Butt.
35	5305-21-107-1317	Screw, Machine. Sil hd, S, anti-rust fin, No 3 BA.
36	1005-21-103-1212	Spring Trap, Butt Plate. (2 styles)
37	1005-21-103-1358	Trap Assembly, Butt Plate. (Alternate item NSN 1005-21-103-1198)
38	1005-21-113-8145	Trap, Butt Plate.
39	5315-21-106-6939	Pin, Straight, Headless. S, anti-rust fin, 2.59 mm (0.102 in) nom dia, 15.37 mm (0.605 in) nom lg.
40	5305-21-107-0338	Screw, Wood, oval countersunk hd, slot, dr, S, phos, No 18 wood, 3.81 cm (1.500 po) fas lg.

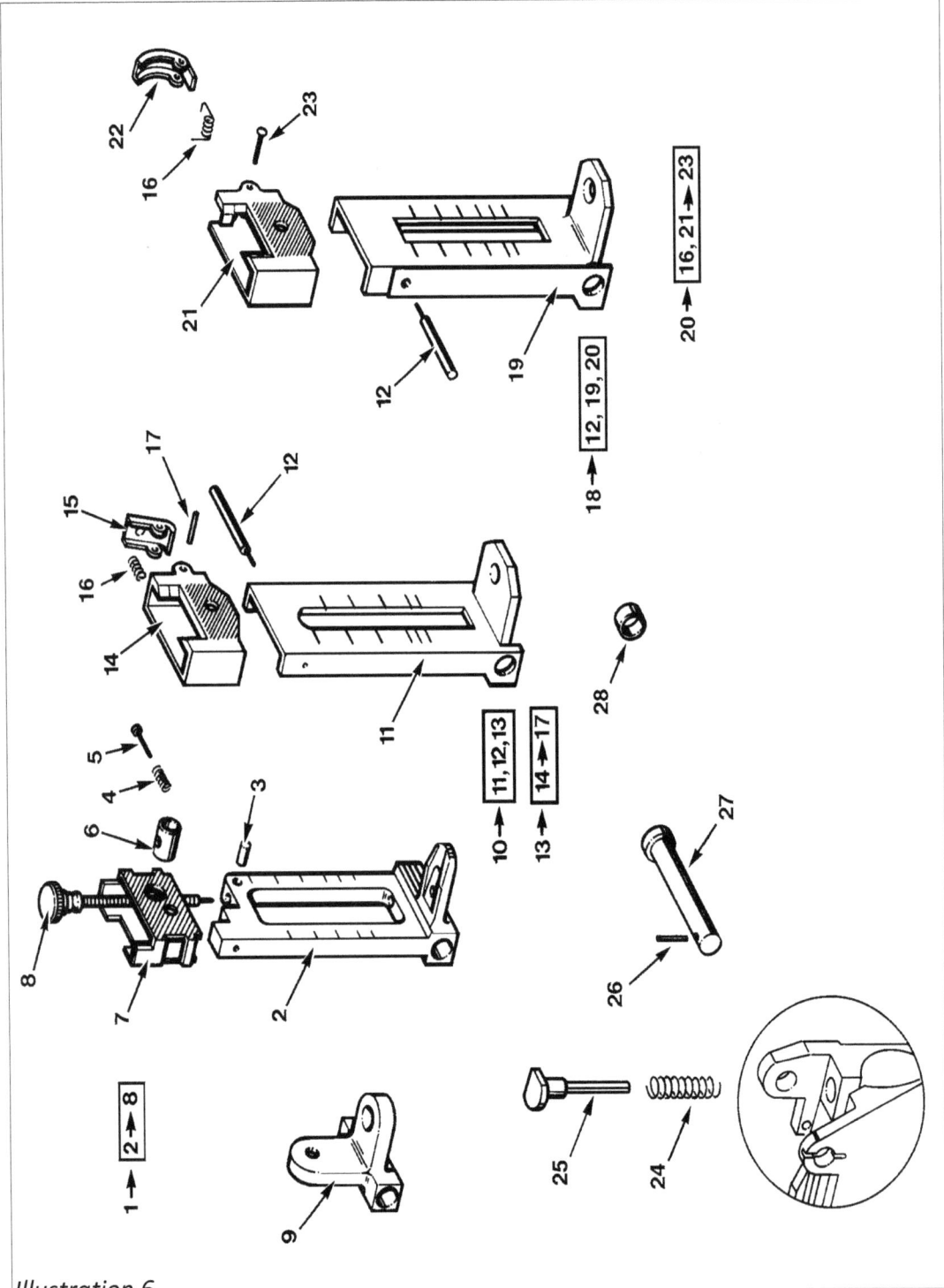

Illustration 6

ILUSTRATION 6

INDEX #	NSN	DESCRIPTION
1	1005-21-103-1411	Sight, Rear, Mk 1.
2		Leaf, Rear Sight, Mk 1.
3	5315-21-106-6934	Pin, Straight, Headless. S, anti-rust fin, 1.42 mm (0.056 in) nom dia, 6.10 mm (0.240 in) nom lg, square ends.
4		Spring, Helical, Compression. S, tinned fin, 1.52 mm (0.060 in) ID, 6.35 mm (0.250 in) free lg, 0.30 mm (0.012 in) mat dia, 4.32 mm (0.170 in) solid lg, 2.03 mm (0.080 in) free OD, must work freely in 2.29 mm (0.090 in) dia boring, 9-1/2 coils, 8 active coils.
5	1005-21-103-4900	Plunger, Screw, Adjusting, Rear Sight.
6		Nut, Screw, Adjusting, Rear Sight.
7		Slide, Rear Sight, Mk 1.
8	1005-21-103-4886	Screw, Adjusting, Rear Sight.
9	1005-21-116-7863	Sight, Rear, Mk 2.
10	1005-21-107-3084	Sight, Rear, Mk 3
11	1005-21-113-8111	Leaf, Rear Sight, Mk 2.
12	5315-21-106-6949	Pin, Shoulder, Headless. S, phos, 20.83 mm (0.820 in) nom lg, 1.63 mm (0.064 in) nom shoulder dia, shk 1.39 mm (0.051 in) nom dia 2.54 mm (0.100 in) nom lg both ends square.
13		Slide, Rear Sight, Mk 2.
14	1005-21-113-8142	Slide
15	1005-21-116-7864	Catch, Rear Sight, Mk 2. (requires spring DDE450-123)
16	5360-21-103-5550	Spring, Helical, Compression. S, blued fin, 2.03 mm (0.080 in) ID, 2.64 mm (0.104 in) OD, 3.50 mm (0.140 in) free lg, cylindrical stock shape 0.61 mm (0.024 in) dia. 4-1/2 coils, must work freely over 1.40 mm (0.055 in) dia rod. (used with catch DDE450-121)
17		Pin, Catch, Rear Sight, Mk 1.
18	1005-21-103-1405	Leaf Sight Assembly, Folding, Rear, C Mk 4.
19	1005-21-103-1119	Leaf, Rear Sight, C Mk 3.
20		Slide Assembly, Rear Sight, C Mk 3.
21	1005-21-103-1406	Slide, Rear Sight, Mk 3.
22	1005-21-103-1120	Catch, Rear Sight, Mk 3
23	5315-21-106-6942	Pin, Straight, Headed, S, anti-rust fin, 1.32 mm (0.052 in) nom dia, 8.89 mm (0.350 in) nom under hd lg, button hd 2.03 mm (0.080 in) nom dia 0.76 mm (0.030 in) nom h
24	5360-21-103-5537	Spring, Helical, Compression. S, tinned fin, 2.90 mm (0.114 in) ID, 21.59 mm (0.850 in) free lg, 0.91 mm (0.036 in) dia mat, 13 coils, must work freely in 4.83 mm (0.190 in) dia bore.
25	1005-21-103-1410	Plunger, Rear Sight.
26	5315-21-106-6928	Pin, Straight, Headless. S, anti-rust fin, 1.42 mm (0.056 in) nom dia, 8.90 mm (0.350 in) nom lg, one end chamfered 1.79 mm (0.070 in) dp at nom 10 deg angle, other end square.
27	5315-21-106-6945	Pin, Straight, Headed. S, anti-rust fin, case hardened, shk 3.66 mm (0.144 in) nom dia, 2.94 cm (1.156 in) nom grip lg, 2.87 cm (1.130 in) nom effective lg
		3.15 cm (1.240 in) nom under hd lg, W 1. 40 mm
		(0.055 in) nom dia hole, fil hd 7.11 mm (0.280 in) nom
		dia 0.64 mm (0.025 in) nom h, W/screwdriver slot.
28		Spacer, Sleeve, Rear Sight.

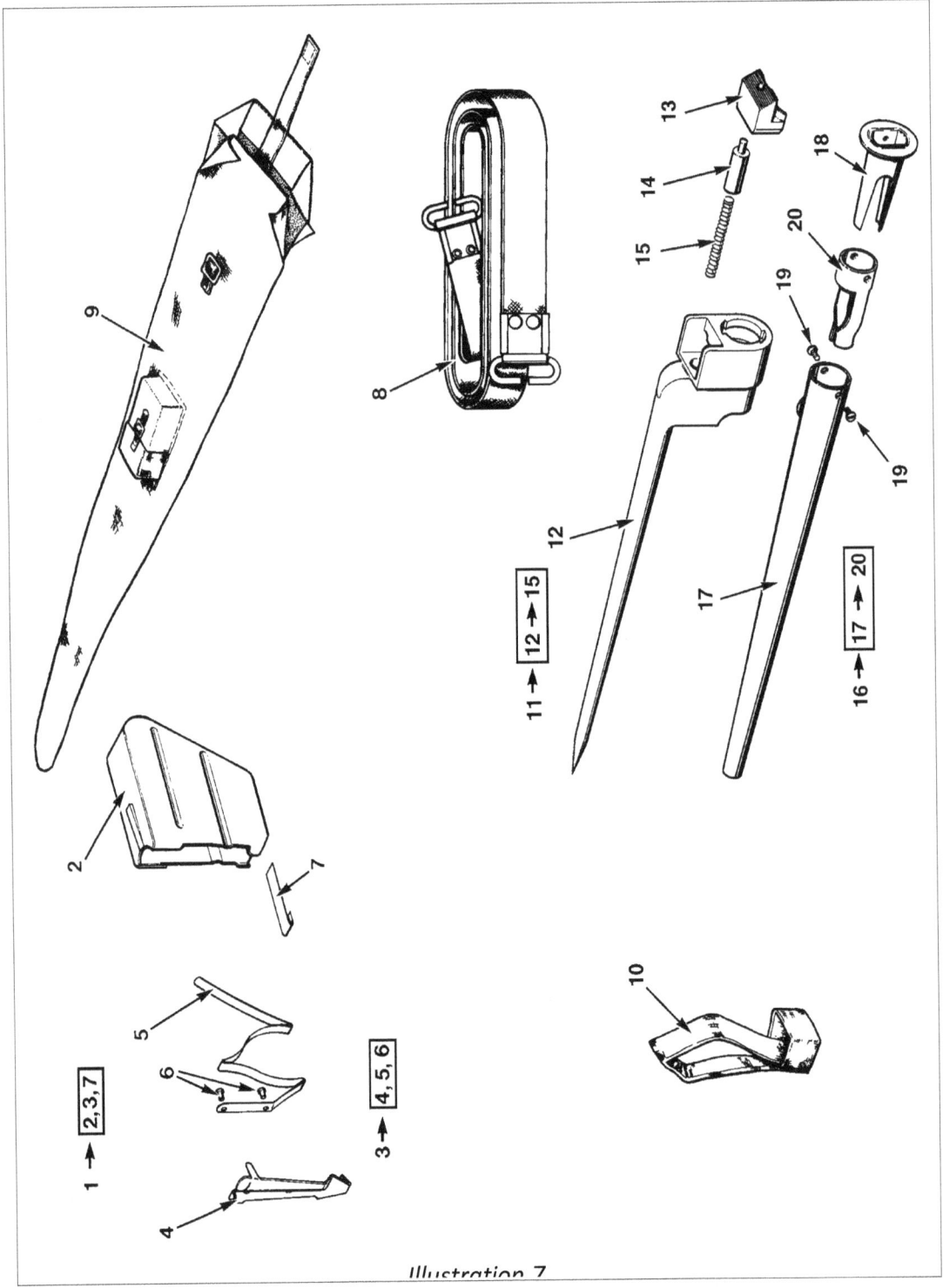

Illustration 7

ILLUSTRATION 7

INDEX #	NSN	DESCRIPTION
1	1005-21-103-4888	Magazine, Cartridge. Cal .303, 10 round capacity
2	1005-21-103-1218	Case, Magazine
3	1005-21-103-1217	Platform Assembly, Magazine.
4	1005-21-113-7697	Platform, Magazine.
5	1005-21-103-1213	Spring, Magazine Platform.
6	5320-21-106-6952	Rivet Solid, Flat Head. S, no surface treatment, str shk 1.85 mm (0.073 in) dia, 2.79 mm (0.110 in) lg, hd 4.06 mm (0.160 in) dia 0.76 mm (0.030 in) h.
7	1005-21-103-5445	Spring, Magazine, Auxillary
8	1005-21-103-1156	Sling, Small Arms, Rifle, C Mk 1. Woven webbing, khaki, open brass loop adjustment.
9	1005-21-103-1344	Cover, Overall, Rifle, Mk 3. Canvas and webbing, khaki, 129.54 mm (51.000 in) lg O/A, 22.86 cm (9.000 in) max w, tapering to 10.16 cm (4.000 in) min
10		Carrier, Bayonet. Cotton webbing, olive green, 13.97 cm (5-1/2 in) lg, loop formed for attaching to belt, W/19.05 mm (3/4 in) loops.
10		Frog, Web, Bayonet, No 4, Mk 2.
11		Bayonet, No 4, Mk 2. blade
12		Blade, Bayonet
13		Catch.
14	1005-21-103-1364	Plunger, Catch.
15	5360-21-103-5536	Spring, Helical, Compression. S, phos or nickel fin, 2.44 mm (0.096 in) ID, 12.87 cm (1.128 in) free lg, 0.81 mm (0.032 in) dia mat, 1.52 mm (0.060 in) solid lg, 4.06 mm (0.160 in) free OD, 17 coils. (Spring must work freely in 5.00 mm (0.197 in) bore.)
16	1095-21-103-6265	Scabbard, Bayonet, No 4, Mk 3.
17		Body, Scabbard, Bayonet.
18	1095-21-103-6460	Mouthpiece, Scabbard, Bayonet.
19		Screw, Special, Scabbard Mouthpiece
20	1095-21-103-6439	Spring, Bayonet, Scabbard Mouthpiece

11

1

10

5 to/à 9

13

12

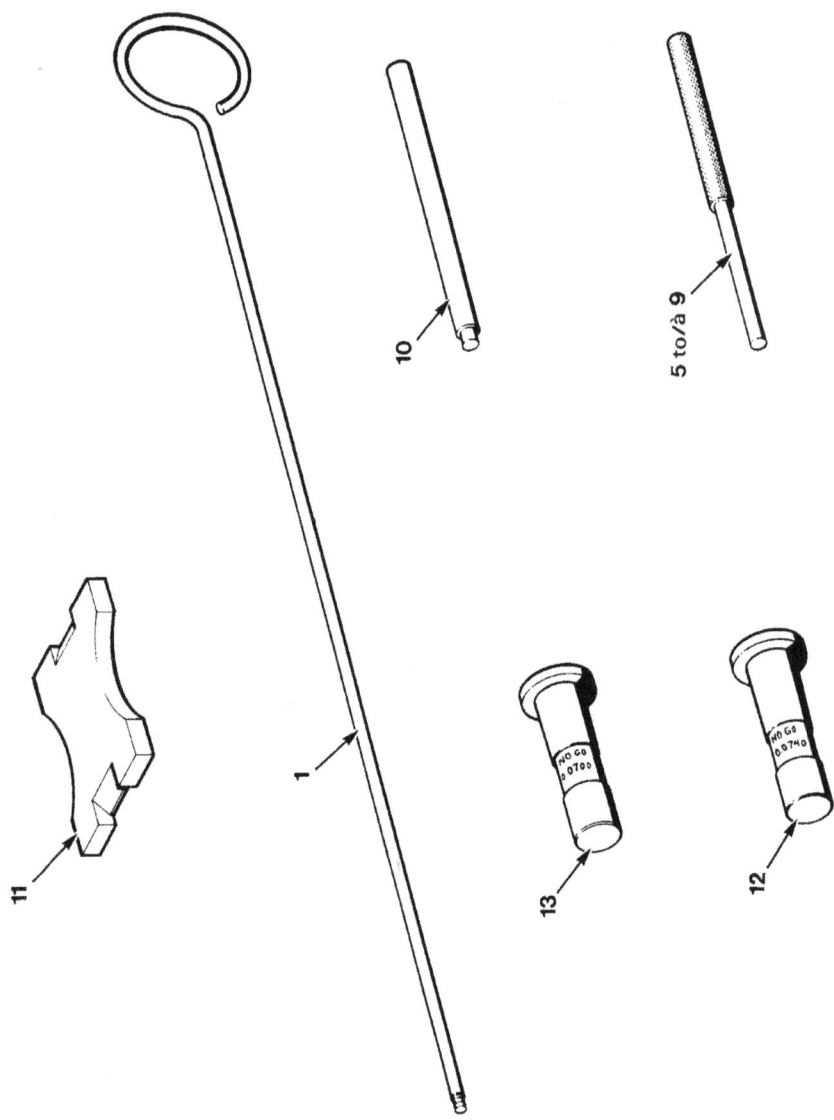

Illustration 8

ILLUSTRATION 8

INDEX #	NSN	DESCRIPTION
1	1005-21-109-2548	Brush, Cleaning, Small Arms. Spiral, rd, phosphor bronze brush 7.92 mm (0.312 in) dia, 5.08 cm (2.000 in) lg, 9.21 cm (3.625 in) O/A lg. 20-1/3 TPI thd 15.75 mm (0.620 in) thk lg.
2	1005-21-109-2521	Brush, Cleaning, Small Arms. Spiral, rd, W/threaded end, phosphor bronze brush, 9.53 mm (0.375 in) dia, 5.72 cm (2.250 in) lg, 9.53 cm (3.750 in) O/A lg, 26-1/3 TPI 15.75 mm (0.620 in) thd lg.
3	1005-21-801-4790	Brush, Cleaning, Small Arms. Spiral, rd, W/threaded end, phosphor bronze brush, 7.92 mm (0.312 in) dia, 5.72 cm (2.250 in) lg, 9.53 cm (3.750 in) O/A lg, 26-1/3 TPI 15.75 mm (0,620 in) lg.
4	1005-21-871-4730	Jag, brass, for 7.62 mm (0.300 in) to 8.99 mm (0.354 in) dia bore, W/int thd 26-1/3 TPI 15.75 mm (0.062 in) dp at one end.
5	5335-21-106-6961	Wire Fabric, Woven. S, no protective fin, 30 by 35 mesh, 0.19 mm (0.0076 in) dia wire, plain weave, unfin edges, 3.65 cm (1-7/16 in) w, 6.53 cm (2-1/2 in) lg.
6	1005-21-103-1327	Pullthrough, C Mk 4B. 3 strands, 3 loops in one end, 127.00 cm (50.000 in) g W/brass or S, weight on
7	1005-21-103-1328	Pullthrough, C Mk 1A. 3 strands, 2 loops one on end, one at centre, 251.46 cm (99.000 in) lg W/wire fabricdia, 8.99 cm (3.54 in) O/A lg, W/screw on cap and
8	1005-21-106-6963	Bottle, Applicator. Plastic, 1 oz 18.29 mm (0.720 in)
9	1005-21-103-1151	Rod, Cleaning, Small Arms. S, shaft, 6.35 mmm (0.250 in) dia 88.27 cm (34.750 in) lg O/A W/str type handle, one pièce threaded end 5.16 mm (0.203 in) dia 26-1/3 TPI to receive brush or jag.
10	1005-21-103-5087	Rod, Cleaning, Small Arms, No 4. S, 6.35 mm (0.250 in) OD, 68.58 cm (27.000 in) O/A lg, "T" type handle, single section, one end slotted to hold swab.
11		Rod, Cleaning, Small Arms. S, celluloid covered, 0.63 mm (0.248 in) OD, 93.98 cm (37.000 in) O/A lg,
12	1005-21-103-5090	Swab, Small Arms Cleaning. Cotton 1.500 in w, 10.16 cm (4.000 in) lg, 100 per bundle.
13	1005-21-103-5091	Guide, Cleaning Rod, Mk 1. S, 12.70 cm (5.000 in) lg O/A, collar at one end thread for locking screw.(not illustrated)
14	1005-21-103-5208	Bit, Removal Tool. S, one end ext thd for attaching to cleaning rod. Opposite end screw threaded and tapered to a gimlet point. (not illustrated)
15	1005-21-103-5209	Guide, Removal Tool. S, internal thd both ends.

ABBREVIATIONS

A/A ..... .As Applicable
A/F ......across the flats
blk ......black
BR ......British
C and CDN ..... .Canadian
cd ..... .Cadmium
cm ..... .Centimetres
ctd ......coated
deg ......degree or degrees
dia ..... .Diameter
Dwg ......Drawing
fas ..... .Fastener
fil ..... .Fillister
fin ..... .finish
fl ..... .Flat
GAPL ..... .Group Assembly Parts List
h ......High or Height
hd ......Head
hex ..... .Hexagon
ID ..... .Inside Diameter
in ......Inch
lg ..... .Long or Length
Mat ..... .Material
Max ..... .Maximum
Mfr ......Manufacturer
Min ..... .Minimum
mm ......Millimetre
nom ..... .Nominal
NS ......Non standard
NSN ..... .Nato Stock Number
or No ......Number
O/A ..... .Overall
OD ......Outside Diameter
OPI ..... .Office of Primary Interest
pass ......Passivated
phos ..... .Phosphated
pltd ..... .Plated
Phos ......Phosphate
PPB ......Provisional Parts Breakdown
Rad ..... .Radius
rd ......Round
Qty ..... Quantity
S ..... Steel
SA ......Small Arms
shk .... Shank
sl ......Slot
str ......Straight
sub ..... .Subordinate
thd ......thread
thk ......Thick or Thickness
TPI ..... .Threads per Inch
UNC ......Unified National Coarse
UNEF ......Unified National Extra Fine
UNF ......Unified National Fine

U/O ......Used On
w ......Wide or Width
W ..... .With
W/E ..... .With Equipment
W/O ..... .Without

MIDDLE
COAST
PUBLISHING

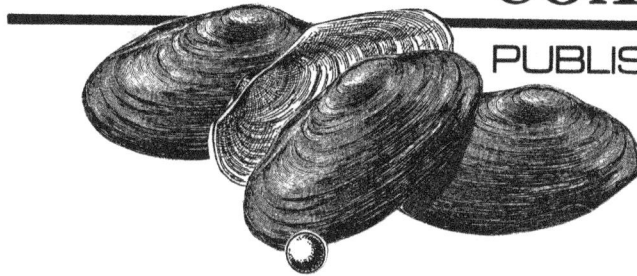

Middle-Coast-Publishing.com

On the following pages is a catalog of our Military Firearms Series of Books, all of which are available at Amazon Books.

FREDERIC FAUST

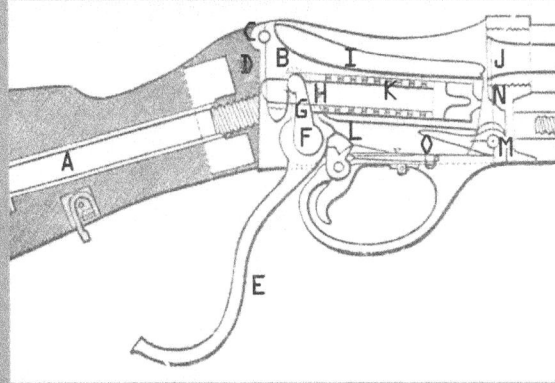

The Lineage of the Martini-Henry Rifle

Facts and Circumstances in the History and Development of the Martini-Henry Rifle

ISBN-13: 978-0934523-56-1

The Martini–Henry breech-loading single-shot lever-actuated rifle, entered British Army service in 1871. Martini–Henry variants, used throughout the British Empire for 30 years, combined the dropping-block action first developed by Henry O. Peabody (in his Peabody rifle) and improved by the Swiss designer Friedrich von Martini, combined with the polygonal barrel rifling designed by Scotsman Alexander Henry. Find out the details on exactly how these rifles work and who was Martini and who was Henry.

K RIFLE MK

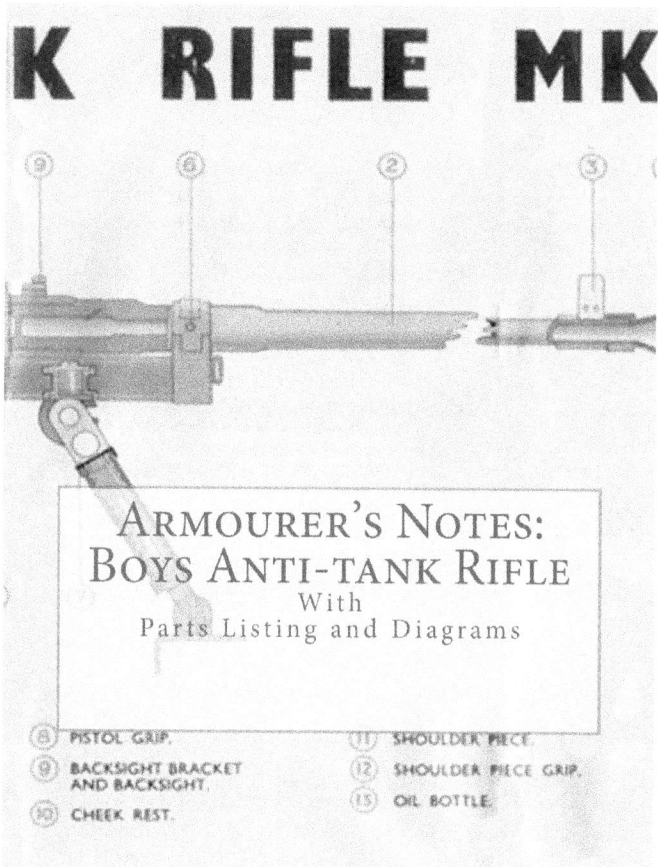

ARMOURER'S NOTES: BOYS ANTI-TANK RIFLE
With
Parts Listing and Diagrams

(8) PISTOL GRIP.		(11) SHOULDER PIECE.	
(9) BACKSIGHT BRACKET AND BACKSIGHT.		(12) SHOULDER PIECE GRIP.	
(10) CHEEK REST.		(13) OIL BOTTLE.	

ISBN: 97809344523-6-46

Armourer's Notes: Boys Anti-tank Rifle explains to troops how to employ and maintain the Boys Anti-Tank Rifle. Coverage includes a breakdown of the weapon by salient groups, showing a diagram of each individual parts and identifying those parts by name and stock number.

LEE-ENFIELD

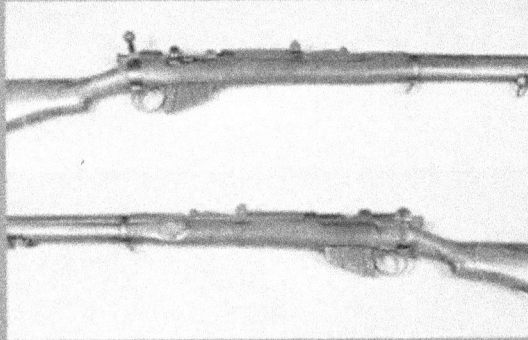

INSTRUCTIONS FOR ARMOURERS

Rifles No. 1, No. 2, and Rifle No. 3 (Pattern 14)

ISBN-13: 978-0934523-11-0

British War Office notes, circa 1931, on the SMLE provide unit armourers with detailed information on how to: Strip and reassemble the bolt and magazine; Clean a rusty barrel, Clear an obstructed bore, Check headspace, Replace a bolt head, Adjust trigger pull, Troubleshoot misfires, Fit a new striker, Blacking sights, and Fit a new fore end.

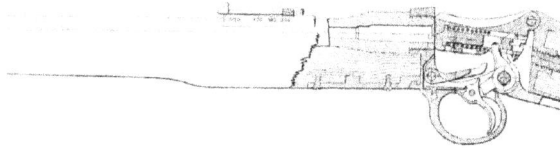

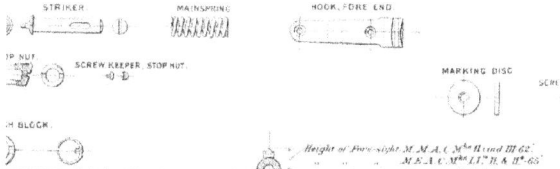

INSTRUCTIONS
FOR ARMOURERS
MARTINI-HENRY
Frederic Faust

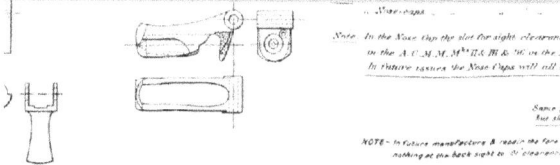

ISBN-13: 978-0934523-55-4

Get genuine Martini-Henry gunsmithing techniques from the primary source, the British Army, circa 1897. This armourer's text tells exactly how to maintain and care for your rifle, from assembly and disassembly to simple fixes to the breech block and trigger.

LEE-ENFIELD RIFLE
EXPLODED DRAWINGS
AND PARTS LISTS

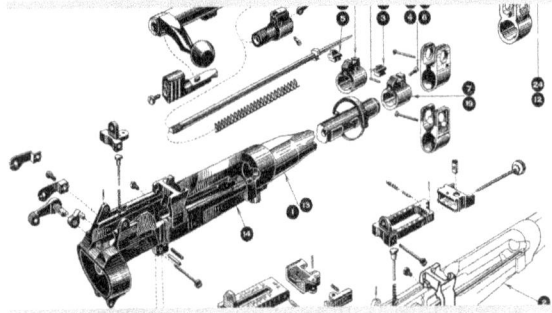

RIFLES NO. 1 MARK III (SMLE) - NO. 3
(PATTERN 14) - NO. 4 MARKS I & MARKI*

FREDERIC FAUST

ISBN-13: 978-0934523-63-9

This copiously illustrated Reprint of a 1945 War Department document shows each rifle by way of exploded drawings of the main components and sub-assemblies. Each part is identified by name and number. Published in large format (8 X 10).

LEE-ENFIELD RIFLE NO. 4 MARK I*

PHANTOM PARTS DIAGRAMS AND PARTS LISTING

FREDERIC FAUST

ISBN-13: 978-0934523-65-3

Built at the Canadian Long Branch Arsenal many aficionados consider the old warhorse to be the best of all the variants fielded during the Second World War. This book contains parts identification lists detailing by illustration, descriptive part name and part number, for all parts of the Rifle, .303 Calibre, Lee-Enfield, No 4, Mark 1 * and its associated equipment including bayonet, frog, action cover, wire gauze and pull-through. Parts are listed to show major assemblies, sub-assemblies, and component parts.

DEPARTMENT OF THE ARMY

FM 23-5
U.S. Rifle Caliber .30 M1

ISBN: 978-0934523-09-7

Profusely illustrated, this Department of the Army **REPRINT** is a guide in the instruction and training in the mechanical operation of the M1 Garand rifle, once described by General George S Patton as The Greatest Battle Implement ever devised. Coverage includes detailed description of the rifle, general characteristics; procedures for disassembly and assembly; methods of loading; an explanation of functioning; a discussion of stoppages and immediate action; a description of the ammunition; and instructions on the care and cleaning of both the weapon and ammunition.

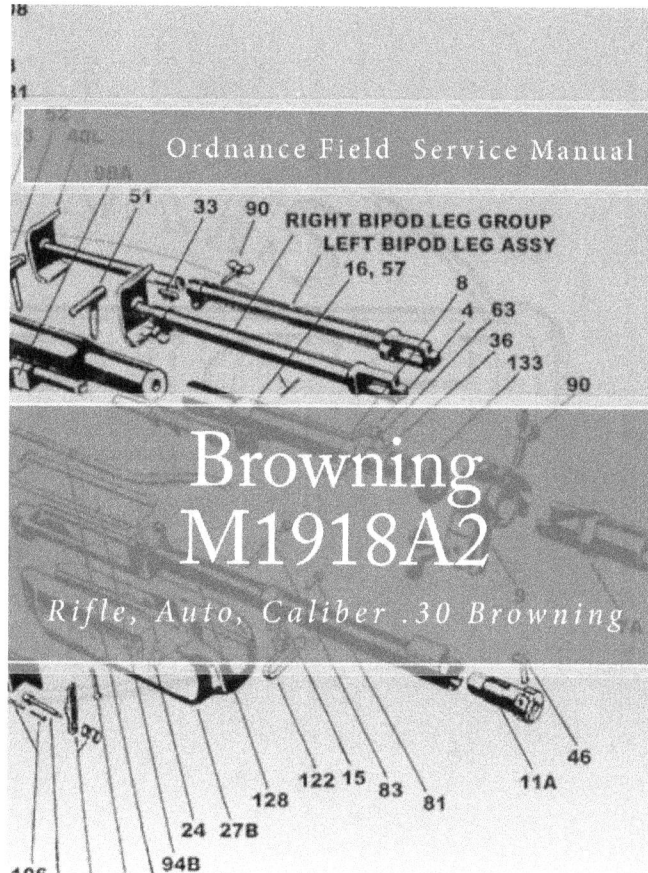

Ordnance Field Service Manual

RIGHT BIPOD LEG GROUP
LEFT BIPOD LEG ASSY

Browning M1918A2

Rifle, Auto, Caliber .30 Browning

ISBN-13: 978-1541187-51-1

This comprehensive, large format reprint of a Rock Island Arsenal manual shows by way of phantom drawings all of the venerable BAR's parts and how they fit together.

U.S ARMY
TECHNICAL MANUAL
Type 99 Arisaka
Caliber .30

Korean War Reprint
Colonel Arisaka
Nakiakiara

ISBN: 978-0934523-68-4
During the Korean War, approximately 126,500 short and 6,650 long Type 99
Rifles were re-chambered under American supervision at the Tokyo arsenal to
fire the U.S. Military M2 -.30-06 Springfield cartridge. These rifles were fitted
with a lengthened magazine well and had a small notch cut in the top of the
receiver ring in order to accommodate the .30-06 round's 1/3 of an inch greater
overall length. The Pentagon rather wisely wrote a Technical Manual for the
converted rifles that addresses inspection of the weapon, care, assembly and
function. This then is that TM.

FREDERIC FAUST

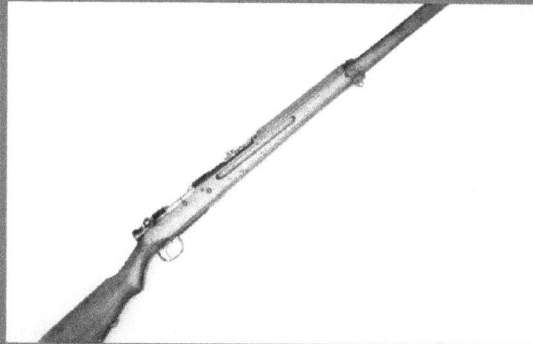

The Lineage of the Arisaka

Facts and Circumstance in the History of the Arisaka Family of Rifles

ISBN: 978-0934523-32-5

The Arisaka family of Japanese military bolt-action service rifles, in production and use from 1897 until the end of World War II in 1945. The most common specimens include the Type 38 chambered for the 6.5×50mmSR Type 38 cartridge and the Type 99 chambered for the 7.7×58mm Type 99 cartridge. Many thousands of Type 99s and other Arisaka variants were brought to the United States by soldiers as war trophies during and after World War II. Find out about the rifle's namesake Colonel Arisaka and learn the fascinating history of this esteemed battle rifle.

EDITED BY FREDERIC FAUST

The Lineage of the Lee-Enfield Rifle

Facts and Circumstance in the
History of the .303 British

ISBN-13: 978-0934523-30-1

This book chronicles the history and development of the family of the venerable
Lee-Enfield rifle, beginning in 1895 with a redesign of the Lee-Metford. On its
pages you'll learn what an SMLE is and what is not, find out which countries
carried it and which wars it fought in plus consult the registry of serial numbers
for Rifles No. 4 and No. 5.

FREDERIC FAUST

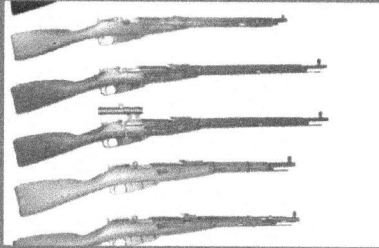

The Lineage of the Mosin-Nagant

Facts and Circumstance in the History & Development of this Battle Rifle

ISBN-13: 978-0934523-15-8

The Mosin–Nagant is a five-shot, bolt-action, internal magazine-fed, military rifle, developed by the Imperial Russian Army in 1882–91 and used by the armed forces of the Russian Empire, the Soviet Union and various other nations.

It is one of the most mass-produced military bolt-action rifles in history with over 37 million units produced since its invention in 1891. And in spite of its age, it has pulled duty in various armed conflicts around the world even up to the modern day. This comes as no big surprise when considering how these rifles are plentiful, cheap, rugged, simple to use, and effective, much like the AK-47 and its variants.

Find out about the parts played by the rifles namesakes Mosin and Nagant. Learn all about the fascinating history and evolution of this esteemed battle rifle.

www.ingramcontent.com/pod-product-compliance
Lightning Source LLC
Chambersburg PA
CBHW081306040426

42452CB00014B/2674